OCCASIONS

OCCASIONS:

Selected Poems

Marilyn McEntyre

RESOURCE *Publications* · Eugene, Oregon

OCCASIONS
Selected Poems

Resource Publications
An Imprint of Wipf and Stock Publishers
199 W. 8th Ave., Suite 3
Eugene, OR 97401

www.wipfandstock.com

PAPERBACK ISBN: 978-1-5326-5247-9
HARDCOVER ISBN: 978-1-5326-5248-6
EBOOK ISBN: 978-1-5326-5249-3

Manufactured in the U.S.A.   AUGUST 21, 2018 *for John,*

for our children and grandchildren

and for the friends who have provided so many reasons to rejoice

and to write

CONTENTS

CONTENTS

CONTENTS

INTRODUCTION

I DOUBT MANY TODAY would agree with Goethe's claim that "occasional poetry" is "the highest kind," but it has claimed a place in every dog-eared anthology. Poems written in private serve public purposes and wreak effects their writers can't anticipate. Poems written for particular occasions—weddings, memorial services, birthdays, anniversaries, dedications, inaugurations—invite us to pause over what is happening, recognize its significance, see it against the broad backdrop of history—personal or cultural—and enter into celebration or mourning or thanksgiving and hope with deepened attention and intention. They bring a liturgical sensibility to the life events we share.

The poems in this collection were all written for "occasions," some more explicit about the nature of the occasion than others. Like all poems, they are acts of attention, invitation, celebration of language, and reflection on what to make of what is given. It is my hope that they might, in their various ways, help us remember or imagine what we have in common.

Perhaps a line here or there will meet some need or awaken a flicker of feeling or open a door. Poems are occasions. May these poems be occasions of grace.

Marilyn McEntyre
March, 2018

I

OCCASIONS OF GRACE

Advent on the Central Coast

Sun falls on grass
as green as April's.
Shadows of passing clouds
barely darken the patio tiles.

Only a breeze reminds us
this is not spring, but a season
of long nights and inward turning.
The purple candle is lit. Three more

wait untouched in a fresh wreath
for Sundays to pass in solemn procession
as the season unfolds. Ancient
rituals survive among all the year's

particulars: a sick friend needs solace,
a project is completed, a child is born.
Once again we lay aside
what has befallen and beset us

to prepare a way for what is coming.
"The time is near," we sing,
"for the crowning of the year . . . ."
Despite fatigue, delays, digressions,

there will be a feast.
We must make ready.

River Walk, January 6

Where river laps the shore
small birds and burrowing creatures
find what they need.

An egret stands listening.
Her quiet stills us for a moment,
and we listen, too.

Home from our walk, and warm,
we reheat yesterday's barley stew
and make tea and talk

while afternoon turns to evening.
Lights on the little tree and candles
mark the twelve days

from Christmas to Epiphany.
At the edge of a year so many begin
with unsettled hopes we gather

reasons to rejoice, having returned
from another edge, peered into a chasm
and seen how even there light

suffuses the hospital room, the face
of a nurse nearing the end of her shift,
the riparian dreamspace

where what cannot be said
may be heard. We know now
how celebration honors

survival, how a turning year marks
what has been saved and given again,
how every day we stand

at the edge of time. How if we listen
we may hear the flights of angels
whose song sustains us still.

🙚

February Again

Just as the year curves into spring
and small buds break
and fill the eye with pink

I wake at dawn and know
you have long since risen
into your own quiet beginning,

tiptoeing past small sleepers
and into the still chill air
with its reminder of winter.

You came on a day like this
as morning verged into afternoon
and leftover snowdrift softened

every sound, your small cry
a heart-stopping greeting, tentative
as the spread of a fledgling's wings.

Every year in the wide wake of Christmastide
February brings its hints of hope, and you
emerge again into what awaits you.

The season, waxing from Christmastide
to Lent, takes its appointed time while
you take yours. Take it, then—every beginning

given—and lift your heart into the new day
again with another small cry
of wonder and another deep breath

of the still fragrant world
that still invites you out of sleep
into a promise still unfolding.

໖

For Sarah, at Sixty

A daughter leaves, a new decade
begins, an ending, an opening,
a turning come at a cost, but rife

with possibility. After sixty
a new urgency drives you inward,
onward, full of hard-won hope:

there is life and time and will,
still, to see what's around the next corner,
peeking above the soil in the next field,

lying just outside the stretch of dreamspace
we call the foreseeable future. What has lain
fallow can flower now, and thrive

where soul-work has been done, effortless,
in spite of all distraction—in you, for you,
in the way of grace. All you have done

has prepared you for what unfolds in spite
of your best-laid plans. So you enter
the elder years where a wide circle

of companions wait to walk this stretch of road
with you. What you need, for now, you may find
in their ancient, gay, glittering eyes.

᳒

Married Every Day

It looks sturdy and sustainable—
fun more finely tuned, and timing
exquisite. You know when

you're near the edge, and that even there
you're safe. You buy shoes together,
and know where to sit for the movie

and what not to bring up until later.
Some things have been worn away—
old uncertainties, leftover fears

imported from elsewhere, not needed
now. You know you are for each other,
and can afford to rearrange

the furniture, the schedule,
the expectations, the silences—
can even afford to step out

onto ground that once was shaky,
knowing you will not sink. What was
separate has mingled, but not

merged, and the long learning curve
continues like a dance step so well known
it needs only the body's memory:

two become one, become two,
and still one. Morning and evening
come again and again, and they are good.

෪

Renewal of Vows

We talk about small things—
which tie you should wear
whether it's recycling day,
whether your phone is charged
and in your pocket
and turned on.

And large things—
how to be healthy
how to love adult children,
be a grandparent,
serve God in gladness
and singleness of heart.

We watch violent films,
and then Jane Austen
or read, together, alone
or aloud, and share opinions
we've shared before.
And fall asleep in chairs.

This is the daily bread
I ask to be given: your voice,
your laugh, your wry asides,

your leisurely walk, the way
you play Scriabin and paint
to Ella Fitzgerald's songs
and talk with children about bugs
and the woman at the bank
about our confusions.

All I do has your heartbeat
behind it. The descant to every
daily occupation is the echo
of your voice in the deep places
where dreams begin. What I ravel and spin
and unspool are never only mine.

All I do draws from the deep well
of welcome you offered when
you invited me to join your journey.
May it be long still, and full
of birdsong and backgammon.
May we speak of small things
with great love.

&.

Celebrating in a Dark Season

Sunlight washes the devastated city.
Crepe myrtle adds its pink to old stone and sky.
Clouds pass in puddles of yesterday's rainwater.

You walk by shuttered green doors.
Every building has its secrets.
Paint peels from clapboard and a roof tile

lies against the lamppost. Masks
for Mardi Gras hang all year in shop windows,
with an air of desperate gaiety.

Everyone remembers the storm, the flood,
the horror, rehearsed now a thousand times.
Death has come, and come again, and keeps coming.

In its wake, in its spite, we celebrate. In its palpable
presence we dwell, safe, in the shadow
of wider wings. The years of your one life

unfurl like a brave banner against
darkening skies. New shoots of gladness
find their way through the dry soil of loss.

We continue what we came for. Music
distilled from sorrow summons us to join
the long second line, beating the drum, singing.

§.

Because it's Not Your Birthday

It's not your birthday.
So there will be no
cakes and ale. Not
much ado about the
many passing seasons
of sun and rain that have
been your story. No
gift-wrap. Or festivity
specific to September.

Let us therefore celebrate
the redwoods that cast
comfortable shadows
on Oakland trails.
And the road that leads
to the blue bay. Let us

propose a toast to every
ordinary day, the memory
of Norwegian skies, a room
rearranged, a paper completed,
wine and cheese and friendship
whose time can't be measured
in candles.

Renewal and Return

Each trek takes you to a new edge.
Each rocky trail offers you its own
silences as you stop to breathe

and be, again, amazed. You find
your freedoms with fierce and quiet
intention. Classrooms and curricula

in abeyance, as Walt might say, and
conflicts that trouble the mind,
over open sea, under the turning

night sky, you do not cease
from exploration. Returning you bring
something of the mountains

with you, and the low notes of monks
chanting, and the scent of timelessness
that lingers like the smell of rain.

Crossing Time Zones

It's always a different time
elsewhere—in Norway, in Spain,
in the mountains where time

evaporates like morning fog,
leaving an exquisite clarity
that sharpens the edges

and deepens the shades
and shadows. Here, time is told
by whistling tea kettles, a white clock,

the rattle of distant trains. Still,
you meet it on your terms. You don't
wear a watch or carry devices.

You walk familiar trails, wait
for salmon on the grill, open
the wine for guests. Moments

are precious. Time is not long
or short, but an old trickster that
lures you into what lies beyond

the hours, beneath the waking mind
where you find you are still, astonishingly,
all you have always been.

II

WHAT IS LOST, WHAT IS FOUND

A Lesson Before You Leave

for a graduating class

Because this day has come, you lay aside
your list of tasks, pin on your mortarboards
and file in, ceremonious, to mark this completion.
Still, here you are in the middle of things:

relationships unresolved, bags only partly packed,
alarm clock lying cracked in a corner, scribbled note cards
strewn by an unmade bed. Finals are over, but still
you wonder what more you might have said

about the English Civil War or the Spenserian stanza,
or methods of subatomic measurement. We, too,
are left with things unsaid after the classes, conferences,
comments scribbled in margins. To one in the back

row we want to say, "Take more risks," to one in front,
quick to speak, "Don't settle for clichés," and to one
whose glance turns downward when we meet,
"There is grace even in failure. Learn what it has to teach."

We want to comfort, congratulate, admonish,
encourage, equip you for the coming journey, confess
what we have left undone. But now we can only assemble
to commend you to each other, to parents, employers,

to God who has held you all along and holds you still.
Finally, the Source of all things is the only teacher
and the only lesson is love. All you have learned
works to that end, is worthless without it.

So practice love. Discover it in the empty lab
as you wait for the slow drip of liquid through tubes,

patient because this matters, though the day
is warm and others have gone home.

Find love in the way a clay pot rises
under your steady hands
while the wheel turns, skill and attention
yielding what is beautiful, and lasts.

Teach love when you ask your students,
who want only to condemn Lear's daughters,
to consider their evil, for a moment, as pain.
Breathe love in the antiseptic smells

of a hospital hall as you struggle to become
a healer at wretched bedsides
on late-night shifts, between exams.
Let love move your hands along the keyboard,

stretch your body in dance, fold your arms around
a crying child, guide your fingers to fasten
wire to wire to make a path for light or heat.
Bring love into the marketplace, the boardroom; insist

on policies that take account of the dispossessed.
Find love in the face of the wandering old woman
you are able to help, the one whose eyes are full of need
and hard to meet. Know that love can be sharp

as the scalpel's edge, puzzling as a prophet's visions,
intricate as the code in a double helix. Let love be
your song, your speech, the energy that fuels your days,
the rest you accept when evening comes. Recognize it

when it comes disguised as loss or pain or sorrow.
Love calls us into the world to learn what only the world
can teach. It is the light we live by. It is the lesson we came for.

For Lindsey, in Her Last Days

I remember you wrapped in purple
one wild October afternoon, color
on color radiant around you,
and your voice a songline among the trees.

I imagine all your songs distilled now,
quieting inward as you learn to listen
to music subtle as dawn, and silent
until we have ears to hear.

I wake early and wonder what dreams
unfurl in you while you rest, your bed
encircled by beings, radiant and ready
to lead you, light to light, urging you

to uncurl whatever still clutches,
and open, open your big heart even wider,
your throat, your palms, every plan
and purpose you've held, and bask

in that light, beloved, beloved,
believing that under all that looms
and lowers and wearies the spirit,
all, already, is well.

For Howard, In Memoriam

I remember your father's scrutiny
that first night, my first
visit. He stirred
his martini, looked
slightly amused, asked
questions. Timid and new at this,
the girl you brought home
to meet them,
I wanted to hide behind you,
so unruffled, so at home,
but I answered him, because
I was a good girl, trained
in courtesy that sometimes took
all the courage I had at hand,
convinced I had not passed muster.

Later, in the garden, I saw him
lean to lift a flower
toward the last light. He looked
at it with the eyes of a man
who has rocked a sick child
to sleep, held a dying animal,
loved a woman, given
sorrow its due—

a gaze that gives thanks
for what it falls upon,
a hand that holds for a moment
what is dear and delicate
and then lets it go, lets it
bloom and fade and fall.

Not in Japan: March, 2011

I woke today not in Japan.
I woke to a blueing sky

and the song of birds still alive.
The deep breath I took

was an act of trust
in air whose particle

contaminants still fall
below some danger threshold.

I turned up the heat because
we still have heat,

and made a note to buy more
coffee, because there is still

coffee to buy. There is no water
in Fukushima. Sixty men drenched

in radiation are working on melting
fuel rods. They will die or lose their hair,

or live with burned lungs and knowledge
no human should have.

We live under the same sword.
The thread it hangs by is bare.

But the day begins quiet in this place,
and beckoning, offering what we need

to learn how to live on a restless earth
between one wave and the next.

❦

After the Fire

Every breath a teaching:
receive, release,
receive again.

In the space of an hour
the wind passes over
and it is gone—

the house, the long table,
the leather chair,
the bed where you lay

awake nights and watched
branches against the sky.
And those are gone, too.

Now you begin
to map the open spaces
your body knew once—

how many steps it took
from desk to doorway,
how to reach without thought

for a glass in the cupboard,
and where to turn at the sound
of the ringing phone.

You move into unknowing,
rerouting the thousand tracks
of habit that seem so like safety.

You knew which drawer
always stuck, which latch

to close quietly when your sisters

were sleeping. The old shoes,
worn to a perfect fit, are gone,
and the chipped mug you loved.

Day by day new items appear
on the long inventory of loss,
and you let go again.

Weeping endures for a night,
and returns, sudden and annoying,
on the road in mid-afternoon.

But in the odd moment, joy comes
without warning. Wrapped
in irony, or curious relief, it brings

its small surprises. It rises
among the ashes. Unsummoned
laughter breaks from a dry throat.

"We learn by going,"
one poet said. And another,
"We shall not cease from exploration."

Feeling your way
into these open spaces
you find what you didn't know

you needed. "Behold,
I make all things new" — old words,
new meanings, new shades

of hope. Grief
dissolves slowly in a sea of grace,
and you are upheld

even in the dark
and the empty spaces.
The burned branch leaves

an open starscape.
What is not there aches
like a phantom limb,

even as you discover
what remains. Already
small birds alight

among the unburnt leaves.
Where helicopters and sirens
cut the air, it opens.

Newly exposed, gasping
in outrage at air and light,
babies take their first breath.

And then the next. Every loss
moves us into new places
of habitation. Take dominion:

make your home here,
on the earth as you find it,
vulnerable and yielding,

where ash feeds the soil.
Sorrow shapes our stories,
leaving scars like runes.

☙

Getting Ready to Go

she said her mother was waiting
could I take her there she was
waiting and would worry she asked
how my mother was and I said
you are my mother she looked

amused then she leaned over
and took my arm she said
does mother know where we are
I said yes mom she knows
she's waiting will you
tell her I'll be there she said
as soon as I can get to the bus
I'll tell her I said she patted
my arm and hummed give your
mother my love she said

※

A Parting Gesture

Small, precise stitches over
and over in the air
are the last thing her hands
can think to do. She looks
past me at something I can't see
in a space near the door
while her hands move
a needle in and out.

I remember watching when
she showed me how to sew on
a button, darn a sock,
repair a torn sleeve
on a shirt that still had
"some wear in it."

When the guinea pig died,
she showed us how to make
an incision, and opened

the little body with
a skill that moved me
from recoil to amazement.

Six unborn babies in separate sacs.
See? She said. And I saw
while her hands gently parted
the mother's flesh.

My mother's flesh
is dissolving now, translucent
and still. But her hands
still stitch, busy and sure,
knowing what they know.

At the Memorial Service

You were the only one
at the service
in bright red shoes.

Your curls shone against
the spray of irises that stretched
vivid and wide just beneath the cross.

Standing in your chair you turned,
scanned the crowd, held my gaze
a moment, stretched, and settled
into the curve of your papa's arm.

When he wept, you watched,
wiped away a tear with your hand,
looked to see that it was gone, then,
satisfied, continued scanning
the dark-suited crowd.

I wonder what you remember
of the darkening afternoon, the fear,
the fall, the long wait for help, the night.

I wonder how often you wake
wondering, in the language she left you:
"*Wo ist Mama?*"

❧

Visiting Hour

She smoothes the fabric on my sleeve,
the sheet, her hair. Her hand
moves more surely now
that her tongue stumbles
and stalls, and loses
direction, mid-sentence.

One eye, nearly blind, is vacant.
The other, though, sees
someone, and she smiles. I am
her sister, or her daughter.
On a bad day, I am just
one of the nice women who visits.

She is glad we visit,
whoever we are.

One day her one eye
twinkles. Head cocked, she peers
at me, curious. "Do you
belong to me?" she asks.

Yes, I say. I belong to you.
She laughs.

"My word!" she says, when I
read in her much-thumbed Bible,
riddled with marginalia,
how Jesus cast out a demon.
She shakes her head. It hardly seems
likely. And some of the Psalms
sound a little alarming. "Maybe
just read a short one," she suggests.

So I do. And she remembers—
". . . all that is within me,
bless his holy name." Some days
I sing a hymn, and she hums.

❧

Invitation to the House of Grief

Come into the dark, and let
your pupils widen. Don't
reach too quickly for the wall.

It isn't there. There is no switch,
no match, only the space
around you. But it is yours.

Step into it and see where
your foot falls. Find
your balance. Accustom your eyes

to the light that comes, slow
and spreading and subtle like dawn,
looking more like night than day.

Remembering Roseanne

She loved Chagall—women and violinists
in blue air and the figure who gazed
from the living room wall, unperturbed

by the swirling energies of a heaven and earth
where there are more things than most of us dream of.
She loved the wild quiet of that world

and of her garden, where comfrey, lavender, chamomile
and banks of lantana greeted her satisfied gaze. She loved
Mary, Queen of Scots—aflame with red hair and courage.

She knew her once—somehow remembered the Scottish court
and the fires of Edinburgh in winter and the long-fingered hand.
She remembered teaching her own hands to speak,

and a laughing aunt who brought her out of hiding
into a spacious self she had to learn to claim.
She loved a man who shared her delights—

finches and tomato plants, a lurking cat and open
country trails and the richness of an unhurried hour
and of a single breath, slow and spacious.

She loved to heal, guided and guiding, to impart
what moves through a willing mind and hand
in a sudden moment of complete consent.

She loved those she called her "dear ones,"
and let them go. She let it all go—the conversations,
the questions, the transporting moments and tears

that came when words failed. What she nurtured remains.
Her place is empty and her dear ones mourn, but she is there
in the blue air with the violins and the floating couples

and the curious winged creatures, loving still and
still in the flow that carries us all onward
to where we started, journey's end and beginning.

☙

III

BEGINNINGS

At the Afterwords Café

So here's where you started.
In the corner a couple lingers
over a dinner long done.

He regales. She laughs. They look
earnest. They appear to agree.
His wine is gone. Her iced tea
provides the only excuse to stay.

A humid walk from work
has wilted her hair. His shirt sticks
to his back. They don't notice
these signs of fleshly imperfection.

Mrs. Dalloway and this month's
Economist lie unopened between them.

Easy to imagine you here
at the Afterwords Café. Red ampersands
in every window suggest conjunction.

The people here read. They talk.
They know about negative capability.
They can define *persiflage*.
They solve the *Times* crossword.
I imagine, inconspicuous among them,
how you amazed each other.

℘

Mother of the Bride

She's doing it all herself, you say—
the flowers, calls to caterers, photographers,
printers. Nevertheless you wonder whether
someone remembered to instruct the flower girl,
trim the wicks, bring the license.

Beneath the babble of detail you hear
the rhythm of ancient words:
bone of my bone . . . daughters of Israel . . .
dearly beloved . . . plight thee my troth . . .
generation to generation . . . .

In long lines a company of unseen saints
leads the procession as the bride waits her turn—
virgin martyrs and unsung couples
who prayed the angelus in wet furrows,
bore their children by candlelight and danced
the hard-won harvest in.

In nearby cafés women and men hear
wedding bells sounding their note
of hope and pause in the riven silence,
unsettled, remembering a longing
they can no longer name.

Moving On, Moving In

Seabirds' cries summon you into an undriven day.
Sand reshapes itself around your feet.

Diving pelicans stitch afternoon to evening
and fly away at nightfall, satisfied. Their going leaves

the air empty and ready to be filled with stars.
Tides recede and leave their jetsam on the pristine shore

to be picked up, turned, glistening, in the hand
and tossed again. You never know

what you are being prepared for, but perhaps it was this—
the keen delight of purple salvia, and new strawberries

to be picked and eaten in late morning sun, the cat curling
beautifully by a window and a cup of coffee

sipped in luxurious quiet. You are rich in what you have
let go. Loss leaves fissures and scars, but now you know

that preparation, and completion are the same. The day's
demands are permissions: Take the walk. Read another chapter.

Offer yourself to the evening alone. Or take the road past
banks of jasmine and wild grasses, across the bridge

to where welcome awaits you. Home is not a place, but a way
of being, knowing where to find the teabags and what to resume.

Root and Blossom

Two trees on a hillside
where living and dying
have taken their turns,
bringing forth fruit in due season,
send their roots deep, tentative,
then sure, of the home they have found
in this hospitable soil.

They stay where they are planted.
Blossoms appear, then crabapples.

Rely on them. Where humans erupt
and go their errant ways, they remain,
called to fidelities we barely fathom.
Remember them. In the long hours
you spend where few trees grow,
in the night when your thoughts bring
you back to this ancient ground.

Come again to lie in their shade.
Consider how they receive the light
they're given. They reach. They blossom.

Making Your Home Here

Let the lake invite you to the quiet deep
and the mountains to wide views, that fill
the eye and open the heart.

Let city streets keep your imaginations
awake to every variety of vendor and tourist
and grey-suited commuter and to those

who have nowhere to go. Let the distances
that stretch between you and the families you love
remind you that the round earth is not

alien, but a home threaded with love-lines
as you pitch your tents on it, where a continent ends
and the wide ocean laps, incessant,

restless, obedient to the constant, changing moon.
We make our dwelling places where we find them,
strangely prepared, alighting long enough

to make them ours, leaving them in
due time. Together, we learn by going.
Where two share the morning or the late

unquiet hours, places fill with purpose
and plans proceed, go awry, or come to
provisional fruition. Make them, and let them go.

Holding each other's hand, walk. Holding
each other's ropes, climb. Following each other's
dreams and deepest desires, trust

that what is given comes with grace,
that love will guide you along its winding way,
that you have, in each other, what you need.

❦

Rooftop Garden: First Season

Kale greens. Beets grow fat and wine-dark.
Carrots spin sun into fibrous orange.
Someone carried soil up these stairs.

Onions open long fingers into morning fog.
Small herbs and winter squash keep quiet company
here on the rooftop while sirens pass below.

In the afternoon one or two leave their laptops
and ascend to this improbable place.
"Put your hands into the dirt," a doctor advised,

and you'll feel better." There is a time to plant
and a time to reap. A time when nature, nearly
spent, needs tending in small places.

Boat-weary immigrants lay bok choy along
the sidewalk's edge. Geraniums bloom
in window boxes. Here and there

insistent chilies dangle on a bush in a half-
barrel. A rooftop is world enough for now.
You don't need forty acres or a mule.

A few square yards, drip line, a couple
of spades and willing hands suffice.
The rest is blessing.

❦

How Way Leads on to Way

On a huge hill,
Cragged and steep, Truth stands, and he that will
Reach her, about must and about must go . . .

—JOHN DONNE

All paths fork and wind.
They invite you on, even
through chill, dark places

where stopping and going on
are equally daunting.
All paths open here and there

onto a meadow or a hillside
full of lupine where stopping
and resting and looking matter more

than hastening on. On every journey
we are joined, unexpectedly,
and share a meal or several miles

with someone who, we later find,
was just the guide we needed—someone to
see us through what we didn't see coming.

"We learn by going," one poet said.
We choose one way, or another, for reasons
we never fully know. What we choose changes.

"Love changes," another poet wrote,
"and in change is true." So take the true
way—whatever way invites you—and let it

lead you through the hollows, over hills,
along the field where a bull eyes you
balefully and into sheltered spots

where you are safe, even on solitary nights,
because, bidden or unbidden, you are held
and witnessed, accompanied and loved.

ೱ

What is Taken, What is Given

The world for which you have been so carefully prepared
is being taken away from you
by the grace of God.

— *WALTER BRUGGEMAN*

Birth keeps happening.
Small empty hands curl
around our hopes and hold

us captive. A child's needs
are teachings. We learn again what
can be taught only from the cradle—

pure pleasure in the body's
many miracles, full-bellied
laughter over falling things.

Small spaces in the heart open
wider as we linger, putting off
what seemed to matter more.

Death keeps happening, too:
fires burn a path through
tended gardens and offices

where good stewards sat at work,
unaware that every page would feed
an hour's ravenous flames.

A young man's body is wracked
with disease, another's, crushed
between metal and slick road.

Fierce as the love that lets us
live to see such loss is the hunger
for life it leaves behind.

Before the backward glance
a new landscape stretches, newly
familiar. That was then—

now is a place of decisions
we do not need to make in fear
or haste. What we know

is sufficient for the day. We
speak the words at hand, water
the plants and watch

for birds in the sycamore tree.
Grace keeps happening. Old friends
invite us, and new ones. We listen

for summonings, subtler now
than when every morning's alarm
set us on a known path.

The call of the moment takes us by surprise.
Every assent resets our course:
Begin now. And now. Begin again.

IV

MOMENTS OF BEING

Appa's Note

It's the deep one.
You pluck it,
and the sound
keeps coming.

The string goes still,
but the note stays
with you, and you
find yourself

listening for it
in the night. Owls
call and feral cats
cry into the dark.

By the bay shore
water laps and wind
plays among pines.
You yawn and sigh.

At bedtime you hum—
a bit of Bill Evans,
the last line of Sunday's anthem,

a phrase from Verdi.
I listen in. I can hear
Appa's note, the deep one.
I can follow it home.

&

In the Borderlands

Afternoons when you walked in
with that look of contentment I loved,
I asked where you'd been
and you said (as though it ought to be
obvious) "At the cemetery."

"Some guy was buried between two women.
They all had different names.
Same kind of gravestones, though.
There's a story there."

"I go there to think," you said.
"I like being there with all those people."

Mornings I would find you sitting up
while your sisters slept. Still seeing
a dreamscape, fast fading as dawn,
you'd recount the night's journey.

There were fish in your dreams.
And long tunnels and underwater caves.
And people who glittered and places
where everything had its own color.

You were an edge-dweller, peering,
fearless, past the partitions that keep us
safe, tantalized by places you can get to only
by going deep into underground caves.

ॐ

What Martha Knew

Busy about many things, she knew how
to cope with others' agendas
and take the days' tradeoffs in stride.

She knew that, unlike her sister,
she was not likely to sit quietly
and listen before the work was done.

But she listened. She heard
his voice as she stirred
the pot, and paused, and wept.

She knew that if he had been there
her brother would not have died.
Even when he rebuked her, her heart

widened and her breath
slowed. So she was content
when he finally blessed the warm bread

and gave thanks for the work
of women who know how to welcome
God himself in the midst of things.

Lear, Again

Reading it again, I want to remember
that Lear was young once, that he had a queen
who bore him these daughters, nursed them
before their gums were broken by serpents' teeth,

that it was her voice he listened for when
appalling loneliness drove him to ask,
"Which of you doth love us most?"

I want to be reminded that Goneril wept
before her tears turned to ash, that Regan
made choices no child should face.

I think how their mother the Queen might
have known Cordelia would be her last,
might have hovered over her cradle,
unburdened womb heavy with death,

how each daughter in turn had to forfeit
some dark hope that she might,
at any rate, suffice.

The lessons it taught me once, when my own
worst follies were still to come, give way to this:

that villainy is pain, extravagant and joyless,
that rage is an untold story,
that every family needs a fool.

&.

Migraine

1

The room slants between walls
that lean oddly inward.
A moment of bewilderment,
then I see you through
air that rises and curls
like heat waves. I squint
and shuffle toward you
between the tables, touching them
as I pass, with slow steps
one might take to be casual.

2

Hovering at the threshold, I say
"Wait." And you wait
while I feel for the wall, my foot
hovering, indeterminate, between
one step and the next. You say,
"What is it?" I say, "I'm dizzy."
We know what I don't say.
We know what is coming.

3

The light hurts, and the air
around my head is heavy;
the breeze has turned malevolent.
Is gas escaping? Can you check again?
I smell gas. "There is no gas."

4

Here is Pier 39, and here the empty
dock and a grey stone wall where I rest,

one hand on it, one on you. There
are the brick walls of Levi Strauss.

You guide me across a street, trolley tracks,
a crosshatched puzzle of paint and asphalt,
past the night-lit bakery, the deserted courtyard,
a restaurant where couples sip their wine.
My steps keep time with a throb
that drowns the gulls and traffic.

5

"Only another block," you say, as I cling
to a mailbox, then a lamppost.
Then we are bathed in fluorescence.
You manage key and door with one hand,
the other buckled round my ribs like parachute gear.

6

Home. I lower my body to the bed and submit
to the thrumming that pulls me inward
to a place I know and dread,
a journey so steep, every step is a fall.
From far off your voice tunnels
through the dark: "Can I get you anything?"
"Water." Hold me. Don't go away.

7

"I'm falling." No, I'm here. Hold on.
The only thing that keeps me from spiraling
into the long vortex, head first, backwards,
are miraculous hands, lacing fingers
into mine, catching me when I turn,
bracing me when I rise, reaching around me,
making a safe harbor while the storm lasts.
And in the morning, in the weird calm
that pain leaves in its wake, lifting strands
of hair, as if gathering flowers.

❦

From the Pacific Time Zone

a reply to Billy Collins' "Eastern Standard Time"

To all you fortunate folk who arise
in the bracing cold of an east-coast winter
morning and fry your eggs and drink
coffee with Billy Collins, enjoying
your solidarity with the staff of the *New York Times*
I have only this to say, from out here where,
as Whitman said, we run out of continent:

It's true that we awaken in a slight but chronic
state of guilt. We have been sleeping while you
finished your impossibly early breakfasts and began
whatever important work (no doubt involving
commuter trains and overcoats and bulging
briefcases) awaited you. We are still stretching
and yawning, gazing out over the Pacific,
silver-grey under a pink sky, watching gulls
and feeding blue jays who have nothing better to do
than wait for a daily dole of peanuts from
the leisurely likes of us. It's true, alas, that we
are chronically behind. Our stockbrokers are
sleepier, and our votes barely count.

Still, as the day unfolds and lies open to the sun
that shines unhurried on these wide waters,
we are consoled by the slow coming of an evening
that will stretch far beyond your bedtime. As we
linger over our Napa Valley wine, here where
ripening grapes sweeten the air, we know
there are still unhurried hours to go before we're done
with the pleasures of the day. While you sleep
candles flicker over our belated dinner

and there remains lamplight and reading aloud—
a little Eliot or Austen—and also Steinbeck—
in a fullness of time that's ours alone—a happy ending
that, sadly, you will miss, slumbering out there
in Eastern Standard Time.

ॐ

Song of the Turtle Tender

Twenty-one turtles, all living together,
some of them out of doors, braving the weather,
some in their water tanks, vying for food,
one in a box, a bit low in his mood,
one eating breakfast right next to the folks
who are drinking their coffee (or decaf) or cokes,
some hiding in shells, some just nodding their heads,
some scruffling slowly back home to their beds,
some scarfing down earthworms, hand-captured with love,
some under the waterfall, some up above,
some prone to explore, some stay-at-home types,
all of them, though they may have little gripes,
quite mannerly, mostly—forgiving, refined—
and all of them (so we believe) of one mind
about hurry (don't bother) and silence (it's good)
and companionship (privacy is understood)
and food (every turtle must fend for himself)
and sunlight (or lamps, if you live on a shelf).

These twenty-one turtles together, they live
in the care of a person who knows how to give
every turtle his due (or *her* due, to be sure),
a person who knows how much turtles endure,
and knows what they crave: the occasional worm,
fat and juicy for breakfast, who knows the right term

to distinguish each one from the rest of his kind,
and who keeps every turtle by name in her mind,
and sends them good thoughts as she goes through her day,
as she grubs in the soil, as she sits down to play
on the cello, the strains of which soothe them to sleep,
(they've come to love Haydn; they know Bach is deep).

They're the happiest turtles in Hershey, PA
and they've much cause to celebrate this very day:
for the birth of a keeper who keeps them so well.
If they could, they'd light fires and toll the church bell
and dance (as they do in the dark of the night,
the way all turtles dance when they're quite out of sight)
and sing in their low, throaty voices, a song
of the fortunes of turtles, tell tales of the long
lives of tortoises, terrapins, aged and hoar
(though some of these tales, one must say, are a bore)
and engage in festivities, slow-paced, but gay
for today, for these turtles, is thanksgiving day!

Working Out the Idea

It's a question that occurs to me
in museums and galleries
and in the fifteenth row when the curtain
goes up and I hear a collective gasp
of pleasure: what muse made precisely this
come to mind? These unlikely colors
mixed into inevitability, the odd abstractions
so inexplicably moving, the whimsies
of wire and cloth on canvas, the turning
of a neck or wrist that defines the difference
between inert and inspired.

In your house you come and go, preoccupied
with plans, programming your device,
spreading your homework on the dining table,
tuning in and out of conversations that must be
mostly background noise for you, immured
in your own unfinished wonderings.

By the doorway a painting stops
departing guests: three bright bands
extend from behind a pillar of cloud,
boundaries sharp and clear emerging
from what seems boundless, held
in a field of energy like notes against
white noise. What made precisely those
come to mind? I carry the colors
with me into the grey afternoon.

In the upstairs hall a chandelier of sticks
and strips of fluttering muslin sways,
delicate and elegant. Mandala-like, it greets
the climber and summons the eye
upward and inward. You did this—
tore the cloth, fastened each lithe dowel
to the next, dared to claim this
circle of space and shape it.

On a shelf a clay hand curls
around what it holds with the kind
of patience hands have when
the mind is made to follow their lead.
The open hand waits and receives: that is prayer.
Closed on a brush or ball or clay: that is
readiness to do the work given.

જ

A Moment Underground

In the subway station
the voice of a flute rises
over a screech of brakes,
the bray of inaudible announcements,
and hushed mumblings of the homeless.
It slides under layers of wool and down
past the numbed drums of tired urban ears
and finds its way into the body.
Not only ears, but skin and closed eyes
take it into where it's a note, received, turns
to liquid and to memory and to breath.

Six Women on a West Coast Morning

All morning we digressed.
Red hollyhocks cheered
from the lawn's edge,
and jackrabbits stirred
the long grass.
Hawks threaded
the air above us.

Story led to story
without plan or effort.
One by one we shifted
our chairs from sun
to shade. Now and then

someone sighed, taking
audible, delicious pleasure
in all this lingering.

How quickly we learned
to share counter space
and quiet and food.
How little it took to make
decisions and perfect coffee.

And how easily even hard
stories were held in that circle,
lying wide and visible
like a quilt on its frame,
stitched over with
sympathy and laughter.

What we carried lightened:
loss, love in trouble, illness,
dreams deferred, and modified,
all of us old enough to know
in our bones and in our bodies
how the urgencies of youth
give way to canny patience,

how joy becomes deliberate,
full and sustained and slow,
fueled by nothing but sun
and a few paintbrushes
and a humming hot tub
and brewing tea in waiting mugs
and women who know how
to say yes, and thank you.

&

Sestina

after Elizabeth Bishop

Quiet in their aquaria, the turtles
blink and paddle while a small dog
sniffs and settles by the fire.
Outside a rising March wind
circles the house: just the night for a poem,
red wine, and a little three-way scrabble—

not the way we once played scrabble,
waiting for players, slow as incurious turtles,
pondering their letters like a poet bent to his poem—
but a game so full of change and quick, even the dog
feels the excitement and the whipping wind
urges us on, and the leaping fire.

It was built with care, this fire,
and slow-growing. A whole game of scrabble
spread its random words across the table, wind
knocking loose boards outside, and turtles
settling into their shells before the dog
curled and the fire crackled and shifted.

On such a night a good poem,
read in word-savoring unhaste by such a fire
gentles the sleep of even a frisky dog
and dignifies the simplest words on the scrabble
table, lying slightly awry like slumbering turtles
on their rocks. It finds an echo in the wind.

Listen into the night wind:
hear how it calls in response to the poem.
Outside, hibernating, two old turtles
listen from the deeps of reptilian dreams. The fire

rises toward it. By the scrabble
table it stirs the slumbering dog.

Trust the sleep of a well-fed dog
and the voice that cries in early spring wind.
Give yourself gladly to friends and scrabble,
and gladly receive whatever poem
comes as you gaze into dying fire
and listen to the night-silence of turtles.

A happy fireside poem,
carried in by a March wind,
should have a dog in it, and turtles.

ॐ

Outside, Inside

Outside, on a perfect day,
indifferent birds, knowing nothing
of species extinction
alight on branches
and listen.

Down the hill State Street
stretches between the beach
and the mountains, elegant
and affluent and open for business.

Inside the sound of pens moving,
keys tapping and wind chimes
in the doorway dispels
passing irritations that might,
if we let them, mar
a perfect afternoon.

§

Men Who Love Mountains

Men who love mountains know
what the earth has to tell.

Ancient stories in striated rocks
and in the bend and whorl of branches

ask only for witnesses. Those who study
or gather samples know what science has to say.

But it is the walkers who go with no purpose
but the going whom they greet: the rocks

gleam for them, the trees bow in the wind.
If you love mountains, you walk

them without haste, taking the pleasure
they offer in due time, knowing

the goodness of snow, and of dust,
of the long view, and of the tree-walled

glen, courteous and grateful
for the birdsong one can only hope

to overhear: their praise is not for us,
nor the distant cries of happy predators.

Men who love mountains cherish fire
at nightfall and withstand the cold

when warmth is scarce. They accept
the steep, rocky way, and the meadows.

Around every bend lies another gift,
some laced with danger.

They know this. They prepare.
They watch as they walk. They take care.

&.

Skill Sets

The quick shift of direction,
change of hands, sense
of when to pass, when
to turn and shoot, how
to defend when you played
defense prepared you
to move from court to court,
with vigilance and cunning,
cross boundaries, play
the edges, fierce and
competitive and, finally, kind.

Winning matters. Loss is costly.
Someone pays. Then
you begin again. You suit up.

All those years you didn't know
it was this you were preparing for:
this day, this sullen, sad kid,
this sorrowing mother,
this impervious judge,
and the knowing
this moment calls for:
the agility, the grace, the logic of Latin,
a historian's eye-view, a sense

of story, of the hard journey
hobbits took that taught you
to take the ring, even when
you do not know the way.

&

Diana

"I got this at the Salvation Army," she says, showing off
her army-green sweater with purple feather epaulets.
"You have to know what you're looking for."

The first time we met my eye caught
on her lace-up boots and pink glasses. I thought,
"I've been away a long time. No one

in east coast college towns enjoys their eccentricities
as much as this." At the interview her questions were
strictly off-limits—the unprofessional inquisition

of a novelist with an appetite for personal facts
that aren't supposed to matter, hungry for a living word
among the dross of dossiers, sniffing out a story.

At the department dinner she explains, "This is
strictly airplane food. I never cook. People come here
for the view. She waves at a row of windows.

Outside the lights of Oakland lie scattered
like jewels flung carelessly abroad
on a mad whim. The sky over the bay is dark.

Strange old women inhabit her poems. One lives
under a bridge. One lives in her car—a dignified
two-tone sedan—and steals food from the market.

I am moved by the sympathy she brings
To squalors and age and poverty,
dementia and cold canned dinners.

She takes revenge on her "wicked stepmother"
in breezy tales that make us laugh, and on the
"waspish sort of fellow" she married

the second time around. "I don't really miss him,"
she muses, "but sometimes I miss the sound
of the toilet flushing at the other end of the house."

She wears her sorrows lightly, having developed a knack
for touching up old wounds with light irony.
She can afford, now, to be wry; she can carry off

peacock feathers and black velveteen jackets found
and rescued from undeserved oblivion
at the Salvation Army store.

&

Blooming

A tiger lily blazes
Outside my window
while I write,
doing its quiet work
while I do mine.

&

One Bee

The bee broaching
this flowering weed
alone in late afternoon
doesn't know the hives
are dying.

Her work lies between
these white petals.

Still, she may have noticed
how few butterflies
color the air.

V

WHERE THE SPIRIT SPEAKS

On the Beach

When you look from here
you can see the earth move.

Hover over the waters
and watch how the Spirit blows

and broods. The sea
and all its creatures still crash

and tumble at the edge
of their silences.

The sun rises and sinks
below the waves. The curved

ocean clings to earth's edge,
obedient, except where

something urges it upward.
The voice that calls

forth the mountains and summons
pelicans and wild geese

says to all things, Rise.
Consent to the upward urge

that calls you out of gravity
into the welter of heat and sound

and color that will not stay,
that you do not own, but may

have for a day, and then
for a night when it falls.

ॐ

Labyrinth—Curtis Hollow Farm

Inward and inward
finding the way
mystery, certainty
stretching today
open before us
letting us roam
safe on a pathway
leading us home,

ancient the granite
fragile the flowers
tough the old grasses
slow the sweet hours
lovely the birdsong,
high in the trees,
finding the center,
finally at ease.

ॐ

On Campus

1

The grassy slope is a gift,
the dry streambed a story,
the upward path an invitation.

2

Faithfully tended gardens
remind the eye to be glad.
Pruned trees make way for light,
swept paths for hurrying feet,
fresh-washed windows
for the wandering eye that seeks
solace, like the Psalmist,
in the hills.

For all who trim and tend,
repair and make ready
these peaceful spaces
we give thanks.

3

The raised racquet meets the ball;
platelets under a lens come clear;
one brush stroke brings life to a landscape;
a poet finds the verb that works.

These walls hold the world away awhile,
open a space for patience,
the luxury of precision,
the small epiphanies.

4

Sycamore and oak,
jasmine, birds of paradise—
these are teachers, too.

5

Light plays on a thousand leaves.
"Love has a thousand faces."

6

In late afternoon
someone in a practice room
comes to terms with Bach.

7

Behind an open classroom door,
laughter—and then, "I see!"

8

So many machines!
May they be user-friendly
and stay in their place.

9

Words scatter like seed;
the Spirit blows where it will.
Who knows what takes root?

10

The earth is the Lord's—
even this busy hillside
part of the vineyard.

❦

First Light

First light offers its quiet
consolation to the wakeful.

In the dark you discover
day, already begun.

The black branches
of the piñon tree
hold night like water.
Moonlight lingers on

rock and sand, slow
to let the earth resume

its dusty colors
after the silver hours.

The last star gives
way, submitting
to the greater light.

Day does not break,
but touches each surface
with deep and momentary
blue, the color of blessing.

❧

Traces

What is wild resists,
as it must. Symmetry

is fearful. Every vagrant
thing leaves its extravagant
and necessary trace. Shards

scatter. Brush and ploughshare
layer track on track, never

altogether new, or free
of old incursions. Work
is reiteration. Discovery

is memory. New and old
do not matter, but only

this moment of seeing
skeleton, surface, edge,
fissure and henge and fault:

unkempt calligraphies seduce
the deciphering eye.

ๆ

What We See By

for the dedication of new windows,
Goleta Presbyterian Church

When light breaks, it cascades in fire-falls,
pools into shades so surprising, you forget
these yellows and greens are the shards of a shattered world.

Each pane of colored glass offers the eye its gift.
Pink and blood red share a common secret,
and every blue borrows something from the ocean floor.

Lines link image to image: the star
leads us again to Jesus, broken for us, here, pane
by pane, each one making an offering of the evening sun.

It is all praise: mixing dyes, measuring space, the careful
work of welding. Even unused ideas stored in sketchbooks
are gifts from a Spirit that loves to play. Now every gaze

that rises from hymnbook to swaying pines outside
pauses upon the old story told again in glass—the lens
we look through upon all that is.

ๆ

Where Light Survives

The earth keeps her secrets
in dark spaces between
sheer walls, in fissures
where small creatures turn

to fossils, deep beneath
the solid surfaces. There
molten rivers flow with no eye
but God's to see the golds,
the reds, or follow their course.

Even among stones hewn
for human use, she has
her ways. Slowly, she opens.
Light comes into dark places.
She accepts the rough caress
of time, and sands blown
by a wind that weathers edge
and plane. Every yielding makes
way for new creation.

Invitation

Come, when you can, here
to where redwoods rise
among the pines and mingle
their roots at the trail's edge.

Come and see the sun
silhouetting the bridge at sunset,
letting the bay go dark
and day blaze and die.

When you come we will
walk by the lake where children
feed ducks. We will watch
for wandering deer among

the eucalyptus, and light candles
and read in the evening.
Time has scattered friends
like spilled jewels across

the continent and beyond.
We visit as we can, sometimes
in dreams. When we can,
we make our way to one another.

We tell new stories, and old ones:
how children have married; how some
have borne their own. How one
is even now being knit in the womb.

One friend faces surgery yet again.
One learns to live alone. Another
plays the cello and feeds a colony
of turtles. A few sequester themselves

in studios to paint. Or garden
in early evening, living lives of quiet
restoration. They restore us, and you,
with the light you bear, and the beat of spirit.

So come. When you can.

www.ingramcontent.com/pod-product-compliance
Lightning Source LLC
LaVergne TN
LVHW021618080426
835510LV00019B/2637